HISTORY RELIVED
The Anglo-Saxons and Vikings

Alison Cooper

Photographs by Martyn F. Chillmaid

WAYLAND

HISTORY RELIVED

This book is a differentiated text version of *The Saxons and Vikings* by Jason Hook.

Conceived and produced for Wayland by

Nutshell MEDIA

www.nutshellmedialtd.co.uk

This edition first published in 2009 by Wayland.

© Copyright 2009 Nutshell Media Ltd

Editor: Polly Goodman
Original designer: Simon Borrough
Layout for this edition: Jane Hawkins
All reconstructions set up and photographed by: Martyn F. Chillmaid

British Library Cataloguing in Publication Data
Cooper, Alison, 1967-
The Anglo-Saxons and Vikings. -- Differentiated ed. -- (History relived)
1. Anglo-Saxons--Social life and customs--Juvenile literature. 2. Vikings--Social life and customs--
Juvenile literature.
I. Title II. Series III. Hook, Jason. Saxons and Vikings reconstructed.
942'.017-dc22

ISBN: 978 0 7502 5864 7

Printed and bound in China

Wayland is a division of Hachette Children's Books,
A Hachette UK Company

www.hachette.co.uk

Cover photographs: Top left: a selection of Anglo-Saxon and Viking food;
Centre left: a woman prepares some food in an Anglo-Saxon hall;
Bottom left: a typical Anglo-Saxon house; Right: an Anglo-Saxon warrior prepares to defend his
home from Viking raiders.

Title page: An Anglo-Saxon village house.

The photographer wishes to thank the following for their help and assistance:
Jorvik Viking Centre, York; West Stow Anglo-Saxon Village, Suffolk.

Contents

Raiders and Settlers

In the year 400, groups of invaders from northern Europe began to attack Britain. The Britons were terrified.

The invaders settled in Britain, building villages and making farms. They became known as the Anglo-Saxons. Four hundred years later it was their turn to be afraid as the Vikings arrived. The Vikings crossed the seas from Scandinavia and rampaged through the countryside.

The Vikings were fierce warriors but, like the Anglo-Saxons, they were farmers and craftspeople, too. Eventually the Vikings also settled in Britain.

▼ Some Vikings built farmhouses like this one. The walls and roofs are made of turf.

▶ An Anglo-Saxon warrior prepares to defend his home.

helmet

face guard

mail shirt

shield

sword

knife sheath

4

A Viking Town

▲ The yard of a house in Jorvik.

In Viking times, the most important town in northern England was York. The Vikings called it Jorvik.

The Vikings captured Jorvik from the Anglo-Saxons in 866. Soon it became a busy market town. Inside the town walls there was a maze of streets. Houses and workshops crowded close together. In the yards, pigs snuffled in the dirt.

bucket of water

thatch

goose

hen

basket

dyed yarn

Traders sailed their ships up the River Ouse into the centre of the town. They sold goods from other countries. Craftspeople from Jorvik sold their goods to the traders.

One of the crafts in Jorvik was making goods from leather. Leatherworkers made belts, bags, purses, sheaths for knives, and shoes. They used a wooden model of a foot, called a 'last', to hold the leather in shape while they sewed the pieces together.

▼ Materials and tools on the bench of a Viking leatherworker's shop.

last   shoe

leather scraps   tallow lamp

bone needles   knife and thread

Craftspeople and Traders

There were many different kinds of craftspeople in Jorvik. Workshops were noisy with the sound of loud hammering and sawing.

bucket   stool   cup   bowls

spoons   spindles   axe   deer antler

The Vikings were famous for their woodwork skills. Woodworkers shaped wood into cups, bowls and spindles using a lathe and a sharp tool. The Vikings were skilled at carving bone and horn, too. Carvers made beautiful pins and buckles to fasten clothing.

▼ Goods made of wood are on sale at this market stall.

Each craftsperson helped to provide work for other people. The tanner made leather from the hides of cows and deer. Then the leatherworker bought the leather from the tanner. He cut it into shape using sharp knives made by the blacksmith.

The Viking traders who came to Jorvik brought goods from faraway places. There were animal furs and precious amber from the northern lands around Russia. Some traders brought luxuries such as silk from China and spices from Arabia. Others sold slaves they had brought from Eastern Europe. Some cunning traders even sold the spiral horn of the narwhal, a type of whale that lives in the Arctic. They told people the horn came from a unicorn!

▲ These items have been carved from bone and antler.

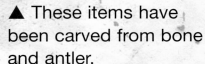

deer antler

combs

bone pins

horn buckles and bone needles

Houses and Homes

▲ A house in an Anglo-Saxon village.

thatched roof

rafters

planks

firewood

buckets of water

basket

Anglo-Saxon and Viking homes were similar. The houses were built of wood, with thatched roofs. They did not have windows or chimneys. This made them very dark and smoky inside.

Each family lived together in just one room. They cooked their food in iron or clay pots, over a fire in the middle of the room. Flat pieces of wood were used for plates. People ate with spoons and knives, but they did not have forks.

There were no store cupboards. Instead, the family kept their food in sacks. They hung the sacks from the walls or ceiling, away from rats and mice.

At night, the family slept on wooden platforms raised above the floor. They made mattresses from bracken and covered themselves with furs or woollen blankets. In the winter, they shared their home with cows and pigs. The animals helped to keep the room warm, but they made it even smellier!

At the centre of every Anglo-Saxon village was the long hall. This was the home of the local *thane*, or lord. Villagers often gathered in the long hall for feasts, singing and storytelling.

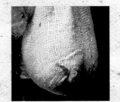
sack of food

storage jar

tallow lamp

cooking pot

spatula

drinking glasses

▼ Anglo-Saxons and Vikings used kitchen items like these.

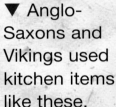

shears

Village Life

Anglo-Saxon villagers led busy lives. Everyone had to work hard to make sure they had enough food to eat, and fuel for cooking and keeping warm.

Children helped their parents in lots of ways. They fed the pigs and chickens, and collected honey from the family beehive.

Women and children searched the countryside for wood for their fires. They hunted in the hedgerows for berries and nuts to eat. Water for drinking often came from a spring or stream. They gathered moss to use instead of toilet paper.

thatching   carrying water

feeding chickens   chopping wood

▼ People busy at work in an Anglo-Saxon village.

The fields around the village were owned by the local lord. The villagers spent some of their time farming land for the lord and the rest of the time growing crops for themselves.

In the spring, oxen plodded up and down the fields, pulling wooden ploughs. The villagers planted crops such as barley, wheat, peas and beans. Sheep grazed in some of the fields. Shepherds kept a close eye on them because wolves were a danger in Anglo-Saxon times.

Travelling craftspeople such as leatherworkers and carpenters sometimes visited the village. Pedlars visited too, selling goods that the villagers could not make or grow themselves.

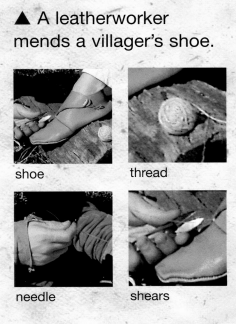

▲ A leatherworker mends a villager's shoe.

shoe

thread

needle

shears

Clothes

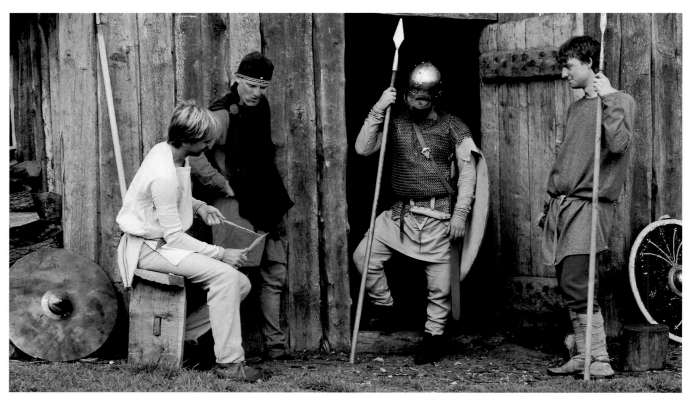

▲ An Anglo-Saxon warrior shares the latest news with some villagers. Warriors wore mail shirts made of iron over their tunics.

The Anglo-Saxons and Vikings wore similar clothes, but they varied in different places and from year to year.

Anglo-Saxon men wore woollen tunics tied at the waist, and trousers called *braies*. To keep them warm, they wore a cloak and fastened it with a brooch at their right shoulder. This meant they could still use their right arm to draw their sword easily. Some Anglo-Saxon men wore woollen or leather caps.

tunic

braies

cloak

circular brooch

leather cap

leather shoes

Women wore an undergown, with a long woollen gown over the top. They hung a useful knife or a small bag on their belt. Woollen cloaks and headscarves helped to keep them warm.

Both men and women used circular brooches to fasten their clothes. Other shapes, such as animals and birds, were popular, too. Jewellers produced beautiful gold brooches, with glass and precious stones set in delicate patterns.

Viking arm-rings were like heavy bracelets. They were decorated with loops and swirls. Some were decorated with 'gripping beasts'. These were fantastic creatures that looked like a cross between a dragon and a weasel.

▼ These women and children are wearing typical Anglo-Saxon clothes.

gown and undergown

embroidered sleeve

belt

headscarf

necklace

knife

purse

child's tunic

Food and Cooking

hearth	cauldron
wooden spoon	clay bowls
clay jug	wooden bench

▲ These Anglo-Saxon women are preparing a meal in the long hall.

The Anglo-Saxons and Vikings ate lots of different meats, fish and vegetables. Many of the foods they ate were the same as those we eat today.

The hearth was an open fire surrounded by flat stones. The women made bread from rye and wheat, and put it on the hearthstones to bake. They cooked porridge and stews in a big iron pot that hung over the fire.

People who could afford meat might have eaten beef, pork, lamb, chicken and geese. Poor people only ate meat when they shared a feast in the long hall. Sometimes they might catch a hare or trap a duck. Near the sea people trapped seabirds and collected their eggs. They caught fish and gathered shellfish such as mussels.

Most farm animals were killed in the autumn because there was not enough fodder to keep them alive through the winter. There were no freezers in Anglo-Saxon and Viking times. Instead, meat was dried and packed in salt to stop it going bad. Other ways to stop food going bad were to hang it in the smoke over the fire, or pickle it in whey.

▼ A table of Anglo-Saxon and Viking food.

dried fish

whey

flat breads

salted cod

sour milk

sheep's head

seabird eggs

rye bread

guillemot

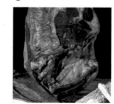
smoked lamb

Feasts

The Anglo-Saxons and Vikings held feasts to celebrate special events. Perhaps the villagers had finished harvesting the crops, or the lord had won a battle.

The feast took place in the long hall. The men hung their swords and shields on the walls. This was partly for decoration. It also meant their weapons were close at hand if the village was suddenly attacked.

▼ These villagers are enjoying a feast in the long hall.

shield

sword

helmet

table

jug of mead

cup

Drinking was an important part of feasts. The favourite drinks were mead and ale. Mead is a sweet drink made from honey.

Wealthier people often had drinking cups made from glass, but most people used drinking horns. These were made from the horns of cattle and were often beautifully decorated.

For entertainment, people gambled with dice and played board games. Some of the Vikings' board games were similar to chess. The Vikings liked rougher games, too, such as wrestling and horse fighting.

Telling riddles was fun. Listeners had to try to work out what the speaker was describing. One riddle went like this: 'I am solitary, wounded by iron/Battered by weapons... /Weary of sword edges.' The answer to this riddle is 'a shield'.

▲ Villagers have a drink at a feast.

drinking glass

drinking horn

Telling Tales

At the end of each day, as it was beginning to get dark, people stopped their work in the fields and headed home. They gathered round the hearth and listened to stories in the flickering firelight.

In Anglo-Saxon and Viking times, most people could not read or write. Storytellers learned stories by listening and remembering them, word for word. The same stories were told for hundreds of years.

The oldest Anglo-Saxon tale that we know today is called *Beowulf*. It is about a Swedish prince, who travels to the palace of the Danish king, Hrothgar. There he kills a terrible monster called Grendel, who has been killing the king's warriors.

The Vikings enjoyed stories called sagas. Some of the sagas give clues about real events. *The Saga of Eirik the Red* tells of a Viking who sailed far to the west. He came to a land he had never seen before and called it Vinland. We now know that the country he had reached was America.

clay hearth

firewood

plucked chicken

log basket

water bucket

▲ A travelling storyteller is
visiting an Anglo-Saxon home.

storyteller

bed

bed curtain

Law and Order

▲ A warrior offers *wergild* to a dead man's family.

wergild

mail shirt

shield

lord

In early Anglo-Saxon and Viking times, fighting was the main way of settling arguments. If a man was killed in a fight, his relatives would try to kill his killer. Blood feuds like this between families could go on for many years.

The Anglo-Saxons made new laws to stop blood feuds. If a person was killed, the killer had to pay *wergild* to the victim's family. *Wergild* means 'blood price'.

Trials were held at public meetings. The Anglo-Saxons called these 'moots' and the Vikings called them 'things'. A person accused of a crime would swear an oath that they were innocent. Sometimes they had to have a trial by ordeal.

The ordeal might be to carry a red-hot iron bar, or pick a stone out of a pot of boiling water. Then the person's hand was bandaged. If the burnt skin had healed after three days, this meant they were innocent. If it was red and infected, they were guilty.

Often, people who were found guilty were banished from their village. Thieves and murderers were likely to be hanged.

judge   criminal

table   guard

▼ A criminal kneels to hear his punishment from the judge.

War

▲ Anglo-Saxon warriors get ready for battle.

spear

shield

boss

helmet

leather hat

Both Anglo-Saxons and Vikings were fierce warriors. There were many deadly battles between them. The Anglo-Saxons sometimes fought each other, too, and so did the Vikings.

Every Anglo-Saxon town and village had to send men to fight for their king when he asked for them. A villager who refused to fight had to send someone else in his place. If he did not, his farmland was taken away.

▲ This Anglo-Saxon warrior is wearing a helmet with a face guard.

Only the wealthier warriors fought with swords. Some gave names to their swords. In the famous tale *Beowulf*, the hero called his sword 'Roarer'.

sword   helmet

Most warriors fought with spears and shields. The shields were made of wood and leather. In the centre there was a raised 'boss' made of iron. This protected the warrior's hand where he held the shield. Lords sometimes gave their warriors mail shirts and iron helmets for protection, too.

face guard   mail shirt

Anglo-Saxons and Vikings fought on foot. The two armies would face each other in a line. They held their shields in front of them to form a 'wall'. Then, shouting and yelling, they charged towards their enemies.

Religion

The Anglo-Saxons and Vikings were pagans when they first came to Britain. They believed in several gods. Later, they became Christians and believed in only one God.

Thunor, or Thor, was the god of thunder. In stories, he often fought giants and dragons with his magical hammer. Warriors wore amulets in the shape of a hammer to show they wanted to be able to fight like Thor.

Another god was Woden. He was god of the dead. The Anglo-Saxons and Vikings believed that warriors who died bravely in battle were carried to Woden's hall, which was called Valhalla.

◄ This carving shows the pagan god Thor holding his magical hammer.

hammer

helmet

In 597, a Christian monk called Augustine landed in England. He had been sent from Rome by the pope to convert the Anglo-Saxons to Christianity. The first person he converted was King Ethelbert of Kent.

For a long time, Christianity and pagan worship survived side by side. Some warriors wore a hammer amulet and a Christian cross when they went into battle.

Slowly, Christian festivals replaced pagan celebrations. Easter replaced the spring festival of the goddess Eostre. Christmas replaced the midwinter festival of Yule.

The pagan gods are not completely forgotten, though. Some of the days of the week are named after them. Tuesday is named after Tiw, god of war. Wednesday is Woden's Day, Thursday is Thor's Day and Friday is named after the goddess Frigg.

▲ This church was built in Anglo-Saxon times.

uneven stones

round arches

Saxon tower

Saxon window

Timeline

c. 400

Invaders from northern Europe attack Britain. Over the next 200 years they conquer England and settle in villages.

597

Augustine arrives in England. He converts King Ethelbert of Kent to Christianity.

600

England is now divided into Anglo-Saxon kingdoms.

780

King Offa of Mercia marks the boundary between England and Wales with a big bank of earth. Today this is known as Offa's Dyke.

787

Vikings make a small raid on Wareham, in Dorset.

793

Vikings attack the monastery on Lindisfarne, off the coast of Northumberland.

842

The Vikings attack London.

c. 867

The 'Great Danish Army' of Vikings invades Northumbria.

871

Alfred becomes King of the Anglo-Saxon kingdom of Wessex.

878

King Alfred defeats the Vikings at the Battle of Edington.

886

The Vikings and Anglo-Saxons make an agreement. The Vikings are allowed to live in and rule eastern England. This area is known as the Danelaw.

1000

The Viking Leif Ericsson discovers America.

1016

A Danish Viking called Canute becomes King of England.

1066

The Normans invade England from France. The long rule of Anglo-Saxons and Vikings comes to an end.

Note

The letter 'c' is short for *circa*. When it is used in front of dates, it means 'around' or 'about'.

Glossary

amulet A small carving, perhaps of a god. It was worn round the neck or among clothing and it was supposed to protect the wearer from harm.

banish To force someone to leave their home for a period of time.

blacksmith A craftsperson who heats and then shapes iron to make tools and horseshoes.

blood feuds Quarrels between families that often went on for many years. Members of one family believed they had a duty to kill members of the other.

bracken A plant that is springy when it has dried out.

cauldron A large cooking pot.

craftspeople People who are skilled at working with materials such as bone, leather, wood and metal, and making the materials into items that people can use.

fodder Food for animals, such as hay.

guillemot A seabird.

hearth An open fire surrounded by flat stones, inside a building.

knife sheath A cover for a knife, often made of leather.

lathe A machine for shaping wood. The wood was placed on the lathe and the carpenter made it spin by pressing a foot pedal. He held a sharp pointed tool against the wood and shaped it as it spun.

mail shirt A type of armour made from many small iron rings linked together.

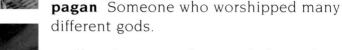

narwhal A type of whale that lives in the Arctic. It has a long, thin tusk that can be up to 3 metres in length.

oath A promise.

pagan Someone who worshipped many different gods.

pedlar A person who travels from place to place selling small items for use in the home.

rafter A large plank of wood that forms part of a frame to hold up the roof.

riddles Word puzzles. People have to try and work out what they mean.

sagas Long stories about heroes, gods and their adventures.

spatula A kitchen tool like a flat spoon.

spindle A piece of wood with a weight at one end, used for spinning wool.

tallow Animal fat used in candles and soap.

tanner A person who works on the skins (hides) of animals such as cattle and deer to make them into leather.

thatch Bundles of straw and other dried grasses used to make a roof.

tunic A long, loose top.

turf A patch of grass with the layer of soil and roots underneath it.

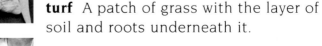

whey The watery part that is left when milk is churned to make cheese.

yarn Thread used for sewing.

Activities

pp4–5 Raiders and Settlers

- The Anglo-Saxons and Vikings came from Germany, Denmark, Sweden and Norway. Find these countries in an atlas or on a globe. Make your own map by tracing the countries in the atlas. Draw arrows from each country to Britain, to show how far the Anglo-Saxons and Vikings travelled.

pp6–7 A Viking Town

- Imagine you have come to the Viking town of Jorvik for the first time to buy goods in the market. What do you notice? What sounds can you hear? What can you smell? Write an entry in your diary describing your visit. Use the pictures and descriptions on pages 6 and 7 to help you.

pp8–9 Craftspeople and Traders

- Look at the photo of the market stall on page 8. Design a leaflet advertising all the goods for sale.

- Imagine you are a Viking trader who has just arrived in Jorvik with lots of goods from faraway countries. In a role play with other members of your class, try to sell your goods.

pp10–11 Houses and Homes

- Imagine you have been for a sleepover with a Viking or Anglo-Saxon family. Write an entry in your diary describing your stay. What did you do in the evening? What did you eat? Where did you sleep? Was it comfortable?

pp12–13 Village Life

- Anglo-Saxon villages often had names that ended in *den*, meaning 'pig pasture'. Tenterden in Kent is one example. Other names ended in *ham*, meaning 'estate', or *leigh*, meaning 'clearing'. Look at a map of your local area and see if you can spot any of these old Anglo-Saxon names.

- Imagine you are an Anglo-Saxon child living in a village. Write a list of all the jobs you might do in one day. Use the information on page 12 to help you.

pp14–15 Clothes

- Draw the design for a circular or animal-shaped brooch to fasten an Anglo-Saxon cloak, or design a Viking arm-ring with loops and swirls.

- Ask an adult to help you dress up as a Viking or Anglo-Saxon villager. You could use long-sleeved t-shirts, trousers, simple dresses, belts, headscarves and brooches.

pp16–17 Food and Cooking

- Design and write a menu for an Anglo-Saxon feast, including food and drink. Use the pictures and information on pages 16–19 to help you.

- Think of a revolting Anglo-Saxon dish using some of the ingredients on page 17. Write a recipe for it.

- In Anglo-Saxon and Viking times, people in England never ate rabbits, tomatoes or potatoes. Can you find out why?

pp18–19 Feasts

• Design a poster to tell people about a feast at the local lord's hall. Remember that Anglo-Saxon and Viking villagers could not read, so you will have to use pictures to show them what entertainment there will be.

pp20–21 Telling Tales

• The Vikings and Anglo-Saxons had only one way of enjoying stories – by listening to them. Make a list of all the different ways you can enjoy stories, for example, reading a book or listening to a CD. Do people tell you stories, too? Which do you enjoy most?

pp22–23 Law and Order

• In Anglo-Saxon and Viking times, most people spent their whole life in the same village. They rarely travelled beyond it. Imagine you are villager in

Anglo-Saxon times and you have just been banished from your village as a punishment. Write down some adjectives to describe your feelings.

pp24–25 War

• Using cardboard and pens, design and make a round shield like the ones used by the Anglo-Saxons and Vikings. Don't forget to include the boss in the centre. You could hang your shield on the wall of your classroom, as they did in the long hall.

pp26–27 Religion

• Find out if there are any Anglo-Saxon churches in your local area. See if you can visit them.

• Use the library or the Internet to find out about St Augustine, St Aidan and St Cuthbert – monks who converted Anglo-Saxons to Christianity.

Find Out More

BOOKS TO READ

British Heritage: The Anglo-Saxons in Britain by Robert Hull (Wayland, 2007)

British Heritage: The Vikings in Britain by Robert Hull (Wayland, 2007)

Hallmarks of History: Viking Longboat by Margaret Mulvihill (Franklin Watts, 2006)

History from Buildings: Anglo-Saxon and Viking Britain by Alex Woolf (Franklin Watts, 2006)

The History Detective Investigates: Anglo-Saxons by Neil Tonge (Wayland, 2008)

You Wouldn't Want to be a Viking Explorer by Andrew Langley (Wayland, 2001)

PLACES TO VISIT

Jorvik, Coppergate, York YO1 9WT
www.jorvik-viking-centre.co.uk/
A reconstruction of the sights, sounds and smells of Viking York.

West Stow Anglo-Saxon Village, Suffolk
www.stedmundsbury.gov.uk/sebc/play/w eststow-asv.cfm
A reconstruction of an Anglo-Saxon village on its original site.

Sutton Hoo, Woodbridge, Suffolk
www.suttonhoo.org/
The site of an extraordinary burial mound in which was found the grave of an early Saxon king, including his treasure, helmet and ship.

Index

History Relived

Contents of titles in the series: